WRITERS' BRITAIN

ENGLISH WOMEN

In the same series

ENGLISH WOMEN

EDITH SITWELL

with
8 plates in colour
and
17 illustrations in
black & white

PRION

This edition published in Great Britain by Prion
32-34 Gordon House Road
London NW5 1LP

First published in 1942 by Collins

A catalogue record of this book can be obtained
from the British Library

ISBN 1-85375-248-7

Colour origination by MRM Graphics, Singapore
Printed and bound in Singapore

THE DISTINGUISHING QUALITY OF THE ENGLISH IS character, not intellect; and in cases of genius it is always character and rarely pure intellect that gives the genius its 'peculiar salt and savour of personal life,' to use a phrase of Swinburne's. Foreigners have declared that the English are more conventional than the people of any other nation. The present writer holds the exact opposite to be the truth, at any rate as far as social intercourse is concerned. It is true that on the continent sexual freedom was more openly admitted than in England, but expressions of opinion in social life were, and are, barred on the continent, whereas in England individuality of outlook is tolerated. The stupid treat it with an amused and semi-contemptuous tolerance, and when they indulge in an outbreak of artist-baiting this is more due to the dislike of the pigmy for the giant than to any hatred for character.

This individuality is present as much in the

CATHERINE BLAKE
Pencil drawing by William Blake

women as in the men. In the place of the peculiar physical energy of the Latin women, we find a flowering of character as remarkable in early times as now.

There was a time in England, as everywhere else, when women were regarded as a subject race. But that phase is over in England: for the character of the English is peculiarly straight and not liable to unnatural deviations: a sense of justice is inherent in it, and a sense of moderation.

This strong national character of which I have spoken is as much a growth of the soil in that most rare of creatures, the woman of genius, as in the woman of integrity whose daily life is a fulfilment of her whole being, but who has not creative genius. Where that genius is present in a woman of England it is a genius of *temper*, using the word in the sense in which we speak of steel having a fine temper. It is a genius of fire and passion, as in Emily Brontë, Sarah Siddons, and that strange woman Elizabeth Tudor, who was as much born to be Queen of England as Emily Brontë was born to write *Wuthering Heights*. The English feminine genius is not one of a luscious glowing warmth, or of sexual seductiveness. In everyday life the English woman is a creature of a broad humanity, tolerant, and with a wide, calm patience and loyalty which is as strong as those great trees which are among the beauties of England. Elizabeth Tudor's greatness, though she had much of the subtlety of an Italian of the Renaissance, was an English greatness, with an English fire and an English strength.

This strength and fire has had an effect of another kind – a puritan disregard for some of the more superficial pleasures of life and aspects of domestic comfort . . . warm fires, and the comforts of beds and chairs we have understood always—but the cooking of vegetables! Each vegetable as much an island as our beloved England, but set, not in silver seas, but in the salt sea. . . each meal the kind which might have been served up by avenging angels at dinner parties in the Cities of the Plain . . . deserts of sand, pillars of salt, wine made from Dead Sea fruit . . . But those meals are now almost things of the past and, until the war put a stop to such activities, English women had begun to prove that they could cook as well as organise a meal. The English-woman's clothes, too, have improved out of all knowledge . . . no longer are our hats, as in Victorian days, a kind of Pageant of Empire, whereon the products of all the colonies battle for precedence.

I would have liked to have given more instances of the flowering of character to which I have referred: to have paid tribute, for instance, to Catherine Blake, the most wonderful wife who has ever comforted and supported a man of genius. I would have liked to have written of those unrecorded women of whom

Catherine Blake is typical, of those women who have never found fame, but whose daily example has helped to civilise our race: the ordinary women in their hundreds of thousands, beings whose warmth of heart and love of country and family, whose unswerving loyalty and gallantry, and gay, not dour, sense of duty, are among the glories of Britain.

This was not possible, so I have chosen a few women among many thousands in whom that quintessence of character expressed itself, sometimes in the acts of their daily life, sometimes in creative work of another kind.

ELIZABETH TUDOR
1533–1603

THIS STRANGE CONTRADICTION OF A WOMAN whose life, seen from one aspect, was barren, seen from another, infinitely fertile, was consistent only in her greatness. That high courage of the lion, and the lion's heart, the lion's rages, contrasted with the subtle mind; that 'pride of the peacock which is the glory of God,' coupled with the knowledge that it was the Queen, and not the woman, that was loved—the love of her people, given and received, together with her heartbreaking and heartbroken loneliness—that ugly face so full of fire, so full of intellectual power and wisdom and vanity, and the exquisite and sensitive hands, that life of duty and magnificence, and that humble and heartbroken death. How can all these be reconciled, one with another?

It was said that she had no heart, though she was at the same time insatiably amorous! Yet her godson, Sir John Harrington, said that he had never seen her weep as she wept when Mary, Queen of Scots, went to her death.

ELIZABETH I 1533–1603

She 'danced high and disposedly'; but in her heart was sorrow and bitterness. ' I know,' she declared to the Deputation which visited her to ask for Mary's death, 'what it is to be a sovereign, what to have good neighbours and sometimes meet evil willers. I have found reason in trust, seen great benefits little regarded.'

Sir Christopher Hatton, who knew her well, said once, 'the Queen did fish for men's souls, and had so sweet a bait that no one could escape from her network.' Harrington declared also, 'when she smiles, it has a pure sunshine that everyone did choose to bask in if they could; but anon came a storm from a sudden gathering of clouds, and the thunder fell in wondrous manner on all.'

She was a woman born to inspire others: she fired men's souls. It is no wonder that Shakespeare lived in the days when she reigned, and that hers was perhaps the greatest age our country has known.

MARY SIDNEY
COUNTESS OF PEMBROKE
1561–1621

In the year 1580, a young man, banished from the Court for his open disapproval of Queen Elizabeth's projected marriage with the Duc d'Anjou, walked with his still younger sister in the woods near Wilton planning a work which still brings back to us a wrecked world—the Arcadia. Sir Philip Sidney and his sister, the Countess of Pembroke, were of an equal beauty. 'She was a beautiful ladie,' wrote John Aubrey, 'and had an excellent wit . . . She had a pretty sharp-oval face. Her haire was of a reddish yellow . . . Sir Philip Sidney was not only of an excellent witt, but extremely beautiful; he much resembled his sister, but his haire was not red, but a little inclining, viz. : a darke amber colour.'

The devotion of this brother and sister resembles that of a later and greater poet, William Wordsworth, and his sister. Together they worked at translating the Psalms of David—a translation praised by Donne in a poem—and after Sidney's death his sister, in her loneliness, edited that work which her brother had written for her pleasure. I say lonely because her marriage, although it was wrecked by no storms, cannot have been one of any great companionship. Her husband, to whom she was married when she was sixteen, was a generation older than herself and had already been married twice.

Lady Pembroke's life was like that of certain great ladies of the Renaissance. 'In her time,' wrote John Aubrey, 'Wilton House was like a College, there were so many learned and ingenious persons. She was the greatest patronesse of witt and learning of any lady in her time. She was a great chymist and spent yearly a great deal in that study. She gave an honourable pension to . . . Boston, . . . who did undoe, himself by studying the philosopher's stone, and she would have kept him but he would have all the gold to himself.'

The tributes to this patroness of learning were many. Spenser's *The Ruines of Time* is dedicated to the lady whose brother was one of the poet's most intimate friends; and in *Astrophel*, Spenser comments tenderly on her likeness to that beloved brother. In *Colin Clout's Come Home Againe* she appears as Urania, sister to Astrophel. Like other learned ladies of her day, she spent much time in translating, Petrarch's *Trionfo della Morta* being one of the works she rendered into English. Only two original poems are ascribed to her, and those with no certainty.

And what of her personal life? She found, I suppose, happiness in helping the great men of her time, and others less great. She had the memories of her heroic brother and of those happy sunny days at Wilton before his early death. There was the long worry about her eldest son and his scandalous love affair with Mary Fitton: a scandal resulting first in his being sent to prison as a punishment by Queen Elizabeth, and then in his banishment to Wilton. There was domestic life, and the search for the Philosopher's Stone. There were the beauties of Wilton. But for the rest, who knows?

SARAH JENNINGS
DUCHESS OF MARLBOROUGH
1660–1744

THE FIRST DUCHESS OF MARLBOROUGH LED A LIFE which was, morally speaking, as much one of camps, of alarums, excursions, ups and downs, and battles won and lost, as was the life of her husband the great General. Sarah Jennings appears at this distance of time like a gigantic figurehead, or the banner round which a battle raged (perhaps more figure-head than banner, owing to a certain stiffness). First she was the centre of one of the rival camps at the court of King William and Queen Mary; then the figure-head attacked by all the intriguers of the court of Anne.

She had a soldierly courage and honesty, a character incapable of lying or of condescending to use tact, which appeared to her as a minor form of lying. With this unbending character she had a violent temper which she made no effort to control; and this, said Lord Wolseley, 'prevented her from calmly discussing any subject, for she could not brook contradiction.'

Was it this incapacity for lying, this violent temper

MARY SIDNEY, COUNTESS OF PEMBROKE, 1561–1621

SARAH JENNINGS, DUCHESS OF MARLBOROUGH, 1660-1744

English Women

and imperiousness which brought about the breach with the Queen whom she had served so faithfully and loved so devotedly? When that breach came it was thirty-seven years or more since the time when a lymphatic, pasty-faced child-Princess had driven in a coach to Water End House, at Sandridge in Hertfordshire, and had made friends with a hot-tempered, determined, quick-moving, pretty child named Sarah Jennings. Sarah had a sister at court and often visited her, so the friendship grew, and some years later, when the Duke of York married for the second time, the sixteen-year-old Sarah was already a member of Princess Anne's suite.

At the Duke's wedding Sarah met for the second time the man who was to be her husband, young Colonel John Churchill, then aged twenty-six. All his life, although he declared that he would rather undertake the whole of his campaigns again than intervene in his Duchess's quarrels, she remained to him his 'dearest soul,' and his truest happiness was with her. For then, he declared, 'nothing can make me unhappy, for I have not the desire of being richer, nor any further ambitions than that of ending my days quietly with you, when the war shall happily be ended.'

This love sustained her during her trials at Court and during the time when King William and Queen Mary tried to get her dismissed from Princess Anne's entourage. But Anne was then as loyal to Sarah as was

17

Sarah to her. The friendship continued until Anne became Queen.

Then, gradually, the break came. Perhaps the determined will that had been so great a standby when Anne was Princess became irksome. Sarah would never allow the Queen to hesitate. 'Lord, Madam,' she would say, flouncing into the Presence, 'it must be so!' Sarah's poor relation, sly, silent, creeping Abigail Hill (by now secretly married to Mr. Masham—the Queen, unknown to Sarah, having attended the wedding), the woman who owed her position at Court, whose family owed their livelihood, to Lady Marlborough, was restful in comparison. She flattered, she did not contradict— and she seized every opportunity to blacken her cousin and benefactress in the Queen's eyes.

Soon Lady Marlborough noticed a difference in the Queen's behaviour, but it was long before she could believe that the difference was to be lasting. Her own straightforwardness and loyalty made it seem impossible to her. But the change had come, and when at last the breach was open the Queen would give her faithful servant and friend no explanation. 'You desired no answer, and you shall have none,' was her only reply to Sarah's question: a reply repeated again and again in the dreadful interview that ended the friendship. Nothing, excepting her agonised grief over the death of her sixteen-year-old son and the later anguish when

QUEEN ANNE (WHEN PRINCESS) 1665–1714

her husband died, can have caused the Duchess of Marlborough so much pain. 'I have always thought,' said she, 'that the greatest happiness was to love and value somebody extremely, that returned it, and to see them often.'

This was the belief of the simple, rather naïve creature whose whole nature was a network of contra-dictions: every act and trait being at variance with every other act and trait. She had this tenderness, together with a violence that caused her to hurl keys, gloves and other missiles at the heads of persons who offended her. She was accused of meanness, but she gave away £30,000 in her lifetime. 'Prithee don't talk to me about books,' she would say, 'the only books I know are men and cards!' But she reverenced Swift and, in her old age, was the devoted friend of Pope, who would sigh, 'Oh, what a girl you are!'

When she was very old, long after everyone she loved had died, she still retained her curiosity about life. Sometimes, at her evening parties, she would cover her head with her handkerchief and pretend to be asleep. But the old spirit was still there and would spring to the attack if she heard the name of someone whom she distrusted: as when some guest mentioned the name of Mr. Fox, of whom she disapproved because he exerted an influence over John Spencer. 'Is that the Fox that stole my goose?' enquired the ancient voice from under the handkerchief.

One by one the lights were put out in the house of the woman who had played so great a part in the social history of her age. But still she remained. She was eighty-four when the last light of all was extinguished and she was at peace.

Esther Johnson —

ESTHER JOHNSON 1681–1728

ESTHER JOHNSON, KNOWN TO FAME AS THE 'Stella' of Jonathan Swift's Journal and Letters, was the child of the younger son of a good family in Nottinghamshire and a lady who was the friend and companion of Sir William Temple's sister, Lady Gifford—but many believe that Sir William Temple himself was her father. After her husband's death Mrs. Johnson and her child went to live at Moor Park, and it was there that Stella first met Swift, she being then eight years old and he thirty. He spent his spare time in teaching her, and she responded with a devotion that lasted till the end of her life.

When, in 1700, Swift settled in the parsonage at Laracoor, in Ireland, he persuaded Esther, then aged nineteen, to live in that small town with, as companion, the good, fussy, kindly, unintelligent, talkative Rebecca Dingley.

Esther's life was one of utter absorption and of a silence like that of death. She lived for her love, and she died for it. She bore all slanders and all conjectures about that love during her lifetime, and she died without breaking her silence. She, who must never be alone with the man to whom she devoted her life, was obliged also to bear that the letters and journals he addressed to her were addressed, as well, to a third person, Rebecca Dingley.

What did she endure when, after the death of Esther Vanhomrigh (whom Swift called Vanessa, and who came into his life when Stella was nearing middle-age), Swift's letters to Vanessa were published? We do not know, although it is possible to guess. That noble silence remained; her lips were unstirred by the grief, the hatred she must have felt.

'With all the softness of temper that became a lady,' wrote the man to whom she had devoted her life, 'she had the personal courage of a hero.'

ELIZABETH LINLEY
MRS. RICHARD
BRINSLEY SHERIDAN
1754–1792

ELIZABETH LINLEY, BEAUTIFUL AS A DARK ROSE, with an innocent youthful loveliness, was famous as a singer even when she was a child. The daughter of Thomas Linley, of Bath, her early life might have been lived in an opera by Mozart: the elopement of the two youthful lovers—Elizabeth, aged eighteen, and the twenty-six-year-old Sheridan (that innocent elopement was a flight from the pursuit of an elderly married rake, Captain Matthews, and the chivalrous young lover was taking his love to a convent in France)—the marriage, the two duels in which Sheridan fought the treacherous and lying Matthews (Sheridan nearly met his death in the second)—the reconciliation with the parents—Sheridan's struggle for recognition as a dramatist—fame.

How sad that the dust of the world should have drifted down upon this youthful beauty, that Sheridan should have been unfaithful, and Elizabeth estranged from him. Yet in those last days when she was dying, in

ELIZABETH LINLEY 1754–1792

the white bow-windowed house overlooking the straw-
berry beds, her lover came back to her with something
of the old tenderness.

SARAH SIDDONS
1755–1831

THIS GREAT ARTIST, WHOSE GENIUS WAS CREATIVE in its fiery and constructive essence, as well as interpretative, was asked by John Brown, the painter, if she thought a part should be acted above the truth of nature. 'No, Sir,' she replied, 'but undoubtedly up to nature in its highest colours.'

'Because,' wrote her biographer, Mrs. Clement Parsons, 'Mrs. Siddons was simple, she was able to give each of her impersonations an extraordinary unity of design, and this we may take to be the root-quality of every new triumph she made. The points of the character were subordinated to the whole, and every action and gesture was related to one single mainspring of passion.'

Her physical genius was such that she could appear a giantess; and a fellow actor, Gage Bartley, described her entering a great archway 'which she really seemed to fill.' She had 'the walk which affects you like seeing a whole procession,' and Fanny Kemble said

28

that, as Constance, she took the earth 'not for a shelter, not for a grave, or for a resting-place, but for a throne.' When motionless she had sometimes the narrow grandeur of an Egyptian statue, sometimes the sublimity of Michael Angelo's *Night*, or his *Day*.

'Her face was seldom tinged with any colour, even in the whirlwind of passion,' wrote John Wilson. That passion was such that she appeared like some gigantic force of nature, tidal wave, whirlwind, pillar of flame. Her eyes were extraordinary, and 'the power of her gaze,' said Samuel Russell, 'made the person on whom it was levelled almost blink and drop their eyes. When she was acting, her eyes could be seen to sparkle and glare at an incredible distance!' Another spectator declared that he had never seen 'so mournful a countenance, combined with so much beauty. Her voice, though grand, was melancholy, her air, though superb, was melancholy, her very smile was melancholy.'

She was alien to comedy, and Colman said that as a comedian she was a 'frisking Gog.' But 'who,' as another contemporary enquired, 'would have wished to see Sir Isaac Newton auditing the accounts of the Mint; or a fandago danced by the Empress of Russia?'

Her private life had the same grand simplicity as her life as an artist. She married, at eighteen, the only man she ever loved, and to whom she bore six children.

The child a strolling actor manager, Roger

SARAH SIDDONS 1755-1831

Kemble, she acted at an early age, and her husband was a member of her father's company. At first the courtship was not approved, and after Mr. Siddons had asked her to elope with him—this she refused to do—he was dismissed from the company and she went into the service of Lady Mary Greatheed; we do not know in what capacity. She seems to have awed her mistress, to whom she read Milton. She also 'spouted in the servants' hall.'

After two years she left, and in 1773 married William Siddons, to whom her father was now reconciled; she with her husband joined her father's circuit.

Her genius did not gain its full triumph until 1784, when she appeared at Drury Lane, although she had acted there with Garrick in 1776.

Her domestic life was calm until the dreadful tragedy which resulted from the love of her daughters Sally and Maria for Thomas Lawrence. Her husband had 'that coldness and reserve,' as she told a friend at the time of the tragedy, 'that want of an agreeing mind (my misfortune, though not *his fault*), that has always check'd my tongue and chilled my heart, in every occasion of importance, *thro' our lives*.' Yet when, in 1804, he drifted away to live at Bath because his rheumatism necessitated it, she paid him lengthy visits, and mourned him when he died. She was in private life as calm as on the stage she was all fire, all whirlwind, or slow tidal wave.

MARY WOLLSTONECRAFT
MRS. GODWIN 1759–1797

MARY WOLLSTONECRAFT HAD, AS SHE CLAIMED IN *A Vindication of the Rights of Women*, 'no fear of the devil before mine eyes.' A woman of high ideals, this child of a wretched marriage, this ex-governess who had seen the inadequacy of the education given to women, faced the world and sometimes the devil, too. She battled to gain for women the acknowledged right to wider opportunities, a freer and less hypocritical sex life, a nobler education, fitting them to transcend petty occupations and aims, and the right for those women who worked, to earn a decent living wage. These claims were made at a time when women had sunk into the position of a subject race, with different and lower aims than those of men; a race to the members of which a decent wage, or an individual outlook or behaviour, was forbidden.

In the age when *A Vindication of the Rights of Women* and the earlier *Thoughts on the Education of Daughters* appeared, looseness of morals was tolerated,

LADY HESTER STANHOPE IN ORIENTAL DRESS
Pencil and water colour sketch by Sir David Wilkie, 1841

ELIZABETH FRY 1780-1845

but not freedom in morality. The tawdry, gimcrack Lady Hamilton was accepted: Mary Wollstonecraft was called 'a philosophical sloven.' But it was an age, too, when the social philosophy of Rousseau and the democratic example of America had awakened man's longing for liberty.

Women, wrote Mary Wollstonecraft, would no longer 'degrade their characters with littleness, if they were led to respect themselves, if political and moral subjects were opened to them; and I will venture to affirm that this is the only way to make them properly attentive to their domestic duties.'

To Mary Wollstonecraft, independence was the main source of happiness, 'Every obligation we receive from our fellow-creatures is a new shackle, takes from our native freedom, and debases the mind'; and this she claimed at a time when independence was held to be unnatural to women. As for sexual morality: 'For what purpose were the passions implanted? That man by struggling with them might attain a degree of knowledge denied to the brutes.'

A Vindication of the Rights of Women is a strange book, with its noble reasoning that is in such contrast to its style and language. These latter bear a strong resemblance to the style and language of *Irene Iddesleigh*. The life of Mary Wollstonecraft was equally full of contradictions.

Her passions were strong and easily aroused; and while she could not bring to them the clear-sightedness which made her book remarkable, she did bring to them the same bad, sloppy and uncontrolled style. In her pursuit of the unwilling Fuseli, in her affair only a few months afterwards with Gilbert Imlay (the father of her child Fanny), and in her subsequent pursuit of that fugitive from her embraces, this woman of a truly noble soul and high courage presented the appearance of a dowdy Dido waiting on the shore for an unwary return. The pursuit and flight were, in all cases, of a terrific speed and insistence, and even at this distance of time we feel almost smothered by the resultant dust.

Yet the anguish of her betrayed love for Imlay, culminating in her terrible attempted suicide, fills us with pity. (Actually, she tried to kill herself twice.) She, who so loved truth in the abstract, could not bear that truth which meant pain: the courage that was so great and high, failed and became lowered when she knew that her theories had crumbled in her own life. She, who so loved life that she had said, 'I cannot bear to think of being no more—of losing myself—nay, it appears to me impossible that I should cease to exist,' endured such agony at the thought of Imlay's faithlessness that she tried to drown herself. We can almost see her walking, as she did, in the cold rain for an hour in order that her clothes would be so heavy with rain that she would

MARY WOLLSTONECRAFT 1759-1797

sink more easily, then throwing herself in the river, only to be dragged back to life again.

We are thankful that at last she found happiness with William Godwin, author of *The Rights of Man*—but only for a little while: a long happiness was not for this fated creature. Mrs. Godwin died in giving birth to the child who was afterwards to become the second wife of Shelley.

DOROTHY WORDSWORTH
1771–1855

THE WHOLE LIFE OF THIS EXQUISITE CREATURE WAS so attuned to the beauties and sorrows around her that 'she made,' in the words of her friend de Quincey, 'all that one could tell her reverberate to one's own feelings by the manifest impression that it made on *hers*. The pulses of light are not more quick or more inevitable in their flow and undulation than were the answering and echoing movements of her sympathising attention.'

She lives for us in those words, and in those written by another and more deeply loved friend, Coleridge. 'She is a woman indeed! In mind and heart; for the person is such, that if you expected to see a pretty woman, you would think her rather ordinary; if you expected to see an ordinary person, you would think her pretty . . . Her information various. Her eye watchful in minutest observation of nature, and her taste a perfect electrometer. It bends, protrudes, and draws in, at subtlest beauties, and most recordable faults.'

She was a household goddess, and under her care and by the light of her love the whole world seemed like home to the great man to whom she devoted her life. She lived by the warmth of that fire which was, above all, lit for William Wordsworth, but which warmed, too, Mary, William's wife, Mary's sister, Sara Hutchinson, and William's and her friend, Coleridge. She thought of herself but rarely, though there is an amusing childish touch of vanity in the letter, written in her sixteenth year, when she was living with her grandfather and grandmother, who made her 'feel like a stranger.' . . . 'So you have got high-heeled shoes. I do not think of having them yet awhile, I am so very little and wish to appear as girlish as possible.' (The letter was addressed to a friend of her own age.) 'I wear my hair about my face frizzed at the bottom and turned at the ends. How have you yours? I have tied my black hat under the chin; as it looked shabby in the former state.'

Her one longing was to keep house for William, and in 1795 this was made possible by a legacy to William of £900. This was but a small sum, but William hoped to earn more by writing, and the brother and sister set up house together.

How happy and peaceful was that life, with the exception of the fleeting sadness about Annette, William's first love, whom he had intended to marry and who bore him a child, and the heavier, blacker cloud of their anxiety about Coleridge, and their final break with him.

In 1794 Dorothy met Sara Hutchinson, then aged eighteen, whose sister was to become William's wife, and their friendship began. In September, 1795, Coleridge first came into their lives, though their intimate friendship did not begin until 1797.

We see Dorothy and the peaceful life at Grasmere, to which they moved in 1799, mirrored even more clearly in her Journal than in her friends' recollections of her. August 31, 1800. 'At 11 o'clock Coleridge came, when I was walking in the still clear moonshine in the garden. . . . William was gone to bed. . . . We sate and chatted till half-past three, Wm. in his dressing gown. C. read us a part of Christabel. Talked much about the mountains.'

But in 1801 the long sadness about Coleridge began. His married life was wretched, and he loved Sara Hutchinson. His letters became increasingly gloomy. Dorothy wrote in her Journal in December, 'We broke the seal of C's letter and I had light enough to see that he was not ill. I put it in my pocket, but at the top of White Moss I took it in my bosom, a safer place for it.'

The sadness darkened, but it was not until the autumn of 1894 that grief and illness drove Coleridge abroad. And when he returned an alien spirit inhabited

DOROTHY WORDSWORTH 1771-1855

his body. They looked, already, at a stranger. Coleridge, although they did not know this at the time, had already fallen hopelessly a prey to opium and to brandy.

But at home, in Dove Cottage, the peace, excepting for the terrible financial worries and the irritation and, in Dorothy's case, anger caused by the reviewers' treatment of William's poems, remained unbroken. There were, too, new inhabitants of that country paradise. In 1801 William married the woman who was already Dorothy's sister in heart: Dorothy became her help, her co-worker, nurse to her children.

She was, indeed, the friend and nurse of all around her. Coleridge came to stay for many months, bringing with him that terrible secret that was soon to be hidden from no one. Dorothy struggled with that illness, as she struggled with poverty and other troubles; but the friendship ended after many vicissitudes and the end was like a death. William, in his anxiety to shield Coleridge, had warned a friend, with whom Coleridge was intending to make a temporary home, about that grievous illness. What he said was repeated, and it was the death-blow to Coleridge's trust and to his love for his friends.

Dorothy was heartbroken, but she supported William in this as she supported him in everything from their childhood to those sad days when the mind which had been so quick and so lovely failed, and she

41

became like 'a very clever tyrannical spoilt child,' though she still had 'intervals of mildness,' and was 'overcome by the old affections.'

One of these intervals came when the brother to whom she made the world a home, lay dying in April, 1850. Her love for him had brought her soul, for a fading while, back to her body.

LADY HESTER STANHOPE
1776–1839

THIS STRANGE, FIERY, IMPETUOUS, AFFECTIONATE creature, who had something of the nature of a meteor, something of the breed and swiftness of a race-horse, seems unreal to us because of the unbelievable yet true romance of her life.

The daughter of the Earl of Stanhope, the niece of Pitt, in whose house she lived from 1803 until his death in 1806, she glittered angrily for a while in the society of London, then, having seen its true worth, left it for ever to become Queen of the Desert.

She had been engaged to Sir John Moore, and after his death in battle, in 1804, her grief was embittered by her feeling that injustice was done to his memory. She retired to the Welsh mountains, then left England on February 10, 1810, taking with her a Doctor Meryon, her maid and a footman. She never returned to England, but, after fantastic adventures, found a resting-place at Djoun, on the top of Mount Lebanon.

On the way there she braved the plague, crossed the desert and faced hostile tribes. Once, hearing that her presence was a danger to the tribe with which she was travelling, she rode out alone into the desert to meet Bedouin horsemen. As they galloped towards her, brandishing their spears, she waited till they were quite near, then, standing up in her stirrups, raised 'the Yashmak that veiled the terrors of her countenance, waved her arms slowly and disdainfully, and cried "Avaunt!" The horsemen recoiled from her glance, but not in terror, the threatening yells changed to shouts of joy and admiration.' These men were, in fact, a friendly tribe testing her bravery.

But before this her progress had been that of a queen, and she had written from Damascus that she was 'the oracle of the place, and the darling of all the troops, who seem to think I am a deity because I can ride, and because I bear arms; and the fanatics all bow before me because the Dervishes think me a wonder and have given me a piece of Mahomet's tomb.' On June the 30th 1813, she wrote,' I have been crowned Queen of the Desert, under the triumphal arch at Palmyra. . . . If I please, I can now go to Mecca *alone*. I have nothing to fear. I shall soon have as many names as Apollo. I am the sun, the star, the pearl, the lion, the light of Heaven, and the Queen.'

In her oriental dress she lived on Mount Lebanon,

LADY HESTER STANHOPE'S RESIDENCE AT DJOUN

studying astrology and the occult sciences and dreaming of the Messiah who, she believed, was yet to be born.

'I despised humanity when I was young,' she told Lamartine when he visited her; 'I won't hear it spoken of now. All that men can do for other men is fruitless; forms and methods are indifferent to me. God and virtue are the foundation of all.'

ELIZABETH FRY 1780–1845

THIS NOBLE LIFE WAS DIVIDED BETWEEN A GREAT work for humanity and a warm and human domesticity—for the latter did not suffer because of the former. Elizabeth Fry bore sixteen children, and those children were cared for by a wise and loving mother.

The daughter of John Gurney, banker, of Norwich, she enjoyed, as a girl, dancing and riding in a scarlet habit. She said, 'I own I do love grand company'; but at the age of fifteen she visited the House of Correction for Women in Norwich, and asked herself, 'If this is the world, where is God?'

At eighteen she adopted the Quaker habit and devoted herself to teaching poor children. In 1800 she married Joseph Fry, a banker, and moving to London became a visitor at a school and workhouse in Islington. But her true work began in 1813, when she visited, for the first time, Newgate, in company with Sir Fowell Buxton's sister. To this man-created hell, in which God must have appeared to the prisoners in the guise of a devil, this great soul brought the comfort of her warm humanity. Of that hell it is not possible to write in the small space at my command: I would only remind my readers that twenty years after this time a destitute child of nine was condemned to death for stealing four pennyworth of children's paints. Eventually, after considerable delay, the sentence was commuted—to what? Transportation to Botany Bay, I presume. This fact alone may bring home to us the sights which faced Elizabeth Fry every day of her life. She was indomitable. In 1817 she founded a school in the prison, under a governess selected from among the prisoners. The state of the prisoners was brought before the House of Commons by her brother-in-law, Sir Fowell Buxton, and Mrs. Fry gave evidence. She formed a committee for the assistance of the prisoners, and soon visitors to the prison 'saw no more an assemblage of abandoned and shameless creatures, half naked and half drunk, rather demanding than requesting charity. The prison no longer resounded with obscenity and imprecations and licentious songs.' 'This hell upon earth,' wrote a visitor, 'exhibited the appearance of an industrious manufactory, or well-regulated family.'

The prisoners so loved her that when they embarked for transportation they went without mutiny, for love of her.

During all this time she had her share of sorrow: a child died: her beloved home, owing to the failure of a business house with which her husband was connected, had to be given up. But, said she, the Kingdom of God was spreading and 'its blessed and peaceful influence increasing.'

By now Mrs. Fry had succeeded in getting matrons installed in most of the women's prisons (before, men had been in charge) ; she instituted committees throughout England and corresponded frequently with prison visitors in Germany, France, Russia and Berlin. Such was her influence in Russia that when, in 1827, the Czar visited the debtors' room of a prison and three old men fell upon their knees asking for mercy, he said to them, 'Rise, all your debts are paid,' though these amounted to a large sum. In Copenhagen, Mrs. Fry spoke personally to the King and Queen about slavery, the state of the prisons, and the persecution of certain sects. In Holland she did likewise. Owing to her intervention the chains were struck off the prisoners in Hanover, and she was instrumental in stopping the persecution of Lutherans in Russia. So deeply was she loved that her journeys resembled royal progresses, great crowds assembling and clamouring to touch her hand.

Nor were these works on behalf of the prisoners

her only activities. She spoke at meetings advocating the abolition of slavery; she founded a Home for nurses who would attend the poor free of charge; she founded, too, the National Guardian Institution for Servants, which enquired equally into the characters of employers and employees, and which provided pensions and a home for old age. Owing to her efforts a series of Libraries for Coastguard Stations was inaugurated.

In 1842 her old friend the King of Prussia, then visiting England, lunched with Mrs. Fry, and on the following day visited Newgate with her and her brother Samuel. Mrs. Fry, we are told, 'prayed very touchingly, the King, and the prisoners kneeling around her, all *equally* in tears.'

Such was the life of this woman who said of prayer: 'It is always in my heart. Even in sleep I think the heart is lifted up.' And who, when she was dying, whispered, 'Love, all love, my heart is filled with love to everyone.'

A Quaker woman c. 1815

JANE WELSH CARLYLE 1801–1866

THE LIFE OF THIS CHARMING, RESTLESS, SELFISH, obstinate creature, in whose veins flowed the blood of John Knox and of 'a gang of gypsies,' the woman who wrote 'I would rather remain in hell—the hell I make for myself with my restless *digging*—than' accept this drowsy placidity,' may be said to have been devoured by the circumstances in which she lived as much as by the greater being to whom she was bound. But that life was not dedicated nobly as were the lives of Esther Johnson and Dorothy Wordsworth; it was eaten and absorbed against her will. She loved, but she wished to love in a way that was more useful to her than to the object of that love.

There were, it is now supposed, tragic and deep-rooted reasons of a physical nature underlying all her unhappiness. But her sufferings were due in part also to the fact that the man whose innate love for her was so tender and on such a great scale, kept that love within his soul, or recorded it by his pen and but rarely

JANE WELSH CARLYLE 1801–1866

expressed, it in the small daily ways that would have meant far more to her. Neither could understand the certain necessities of the other. Jane could not understand that Carlyle must be alone during his working hours, nor could she understand the need of the exhausted man for silence. Carlyle could not understand Jane's vanity and her need for flattery. He could understand, but often forgot, that natures are weak.

Jane Welsh, as a girl, was surrounded by admirers not only of her undeniable beauty but of her supposed talents. 'Mrs. Carlyle would have been a writer had it not been for Carlyle,' exclaimed later admirers; but in reality her gifts were those of a young woman of intelligence and of shrewdness, but of no creative ability. Gay and charming, she had always ruled her world. Then she married a man in the light of whose genius her own small charming gifts were of no more importance than the flame of a candle in daylight; a man, too, whose selfishness was as great as it was unconscious.

Henceforth she had two tasks in life. The first, was thinking about herself; and this duty, self-imposed, was congenial to her though not to Carlyle. The second was thinking about Carlyle, and this task, imposed by Carlyle, seemed to her less agreeable. She could not believe that she was ever at fault. And she could, and did, complain about Carlyle to her friends. Life at the Craig (an early home) was undoubtedly bleak; a life of poverty and hard, tiring domestic tasks, and of unceasing worry. Then the pair came to London and the great man's fame blazed into increasing splendour. But life for Jane was not really changed. Dogs barked, young persons played the piano and murdered Carlyle's unborn work, Carlyle walked about the house with his fingers in his ears. It was obvious that in order to protect him from the noise his room must be changed. It was. And as soon as it was changed, fresh dogs incompetent pianists and ceaseless whistles became clamorous. Jane was blind and dizzy and sick from those headaches which had begun already to undermine her health, but plasterers, whitewashers and bricklayers must be interviewed, and must hammer. Carlyle walked in and out of his wife's room grumbling, or was silent for hours. Carlyle had bilious attacks, crossing Jane's headaches, and cutting them in two: 'Ah me!' he wrote in his diary, 'If I were only a little healthier!'

A friend urged Carlyle to 'bring his blooming Eve out of his blasted Paradise.' But in the blasted Paradise she remained and, in her shabby clothes, watched the innocent Carlyle being pursued by fashionably dressed great ladies. And above all these troubles loomed the influence of Lady Harriet Baring (whose husband afterwards became Lord Ashburton)—the woman of whom Carlyle wrote that she had 'the soul of a Captainness.'

She had, and Mrs. Carlyle was to find the truth of

the assertion. Lady Harriet 'preferred the society of men,' but she was kind to the great man's shabby little wife. Certain and assured in position and in soul, she ignored even the most open resentment.

Carlyle was in constant attendance upon her. She was consulted about, and managed, everything. No attention must be paid, she decided, to Mrs. Carlyle's headaches: but she must be forced to lead a healthier life.

In 1855 she died, to Carlyle's great sorrow. 'Her work,' he wrote, 'call it grand and noble endurance of want of work, is all done.'

Mrs. Carlyle, who had never been called upon to show a grand endurance of want of work, was unsympathetic. She had grown harder, and was, too, backed up in her feeling of injury by the flatterers whom she had admitted, in her loneliness, to intimacy; and above all, by a hysterical young woman, Miss Geraldine Jewsbury, with whom she had formed a disagreeable friendship.

In 1863, following a terrible accident, the seriousness of which must be kept from Carlyle lest it should worry him, Jane's ever-increasing illness became a universal disease of the nerves, bringing, as her husband wrote, 'such a deluge of unutterable, unavoidable pain as I had never seen or dreamt of.' Narcotics had no effect. Yet she was able, from time to time, to go out. It was on

THOMAS CARLYLE
Pen and ink drawing by C. B. Birch

one of these rare excursions that the coachman, turning round for an order, saw that Jane Carlyle had died: alone, as she had lived.

'Weak little darling,' wrote the heart-broken man who had loved her, 'thy sleep is now unbroken . . . And nobody more in this world will wake for my wakefulness.'

And we remember that tragic letter written to her in 1858. 'My poor little Jeanie, my poor ever-true life-partner. We have had a sore life-pilgrimage together, much bad road . . . little like what I could have wished for thee . . . oh, forgive me for what I have thoughtlessly done and omitted . . . far, far at all times from the poor purpose of my mind.'

GRACE DARLING 1815–1842

O<small>N</small> S<small>EPTEMBER THE</small> 7<small>TH</small>, 1838, <small>AT THE HEIGHT OF</small> the Scottish season, the *Forfarshire*, the greatest steamship known to the seas of North Britain, in this year that saw the beginning of transit by steam, left Hull for Dundee loaded with rich tourists returning from their holidays, and merchants and their wives. She left Hull in good weather, but before next morning was in the midst of the worst storm known on that coast for a generation.

At four o'clock on the morning of the 8th, Grace, the twenty-two-year-old daughter of William Darling, keeper of the Longstone Light on one of the wild and savage Farne Islands off the coast of Northumberland, climbed the lantern stair of the lighthouse after the night's watch.

Her father and grandfather had both been lighthouse keepers. Her mother came of an ancient knightly family who had held great estates in the 14th century, and a member of which had been Constable of Bamburgh in 1323.

All Grace's life had been spent among these savage surroundings. The only flowers she knew were those grown on the sheltering ledge of a cliff, whose soil was the droppings made by sea-birds. 'Such land,' wrote her biographer, Constance Smedley, 'as gave her footing amidst the waste of waves, partook of the turbulent forces that for ever surged about it.' For this was the land that had been ravaged by Vikings, the savage country where early Christianity had warred against the forces of black magic. In winter, when meat was difficult to come by, teal, widgeon and wild duck replaced it: poultry could not be kept because of the hurricane-like winds, so sea-birds' eggs were eaten and the down from eider-ducks was collected for pillows, mattresses and covers. As for their home (the rooms of the lighthouse were circular), in one room bunks were built in round the walls. In another room were two shelves of stuffed sea-birds and Mrs. Darling's spinning wheel. And for occupation there was sewing and knitting for Grace's parents and eight brothers and sisters, and there were books; books of Divinity, Baxter, Hervey, and Milton's Paradise Lost, with books of geography and travels, and many maps.

Now, looking out of her window, Grace saw an enormous black hulk on the Harker's Rock . . . 'but owing to the Darkness,' as her father wrote to Trinity House, she 'could not observe any person on the wreck.'

GRACE DARLING 1815–1842

Yet there might be people clinging to that wreck, and it seemed to Grace the natural thing to take the cobble and to row over those impossible seas to their aid. Her father knew that it was absolutely hopeless to take the cobble out in that gale and over those submerged shoals and sunken rocks. It took three men to row that cobble in ordinary rough weather. Grace's brothers were on the mainland and she, the only available help for her father, was a young girl of five feet two, with small wrists. But Grace said if her father would not go she would go alone. And they went—Grace in her gown of green and white muslin, with a small cape; her father in his seaman's clothes. How they reached the rock will remain a mystery, but reach it they did, to be confronted with the desperate and terrified survivors of that frightful wreck fighting for the boat and safety. It had seemed impossible that the cobble should return, but it did return. It had seemed beyond hope that any survivors from the actual wreck could be rescued, but they were. Grace Darling and her father had fought their battle against the sea and had won.

To the last day of her life Grace Darling could not see that she had done anything extraordinary. She was the daughter and granddaughter of lighthouse keepers. Her father had saved hundreds of lives before this wreck. But she became the pride of the nation.

Many portraits were made of her; she was pestered

to give locks of her hair; eulogies and gifts were show-
ered upon her. She was given a silver-gilt watch, she
was given a small annuity. But she had been promised
a dress of real silk and this never reached her: and all
her life she had longed for a real silk dress.

The peace of those happy days in the Lighthouse
was gone. She was only twenty-seven when she died.
The grateful nation said her death was due to exposure
during that terrible dawn. But her family knew different. Grace was worn out; the wild creature had been
worried into her grave by starers.

EMILY BRONTË 1818–1848

THE LIFE OF THIS WOMAN OF GENIUS IS LIKE THAT of the wind and the rain, knowing no incidents and but few landmarks. There was the Crow Hill Flood, when she was six, which brought before her eyes the vision of Judgment Day. Charlotte wrote of Anne that 'the pillar of a cloud glided constantly before her eyes; she even waited at the foot of a secret Sinai, listening in her heart to the voice of a trumpet sounding long and waxing louder.' But this was even more true of Emily. Then there was the night when poor, wasted, disappointed Branwell, dying of consumption, set his bed on fire and Emily extinguished it and quieted his fears.

These were incidents, but apart from these that wild life was lived in the heart and the mind. The publication of *Poems by Currer, Ellis, and Acton Bell* (a publication paid for out of their own pockets) and the infinitely more important appearance of *Wuthering Heights* in 1847, these were the events of her life.

GRACE DARLING AND HER FATHER SAVING THE
SHIPWRECKED CREW, SEPTEMBER 8TH, 1838
Water colour by William Bell Scott

GEORGE ELIOT 1819-1880

Comfortable people were disturbed by the taciturnity of this young nobody. 'A Miss Brontë was here long ago,' was the reply to enquiries about a nineteen-year-old teacher who came to Law Hill, Southouram. An engineer working in the district could only see that the three Miss Brontës were 'distrait and distant, large of nose, small of figure, red of hair, prominent of spectacles; showing great intellectual ability, but with eyes constantly cast down, very silent, painfully retiring.'

As for Emily's visit to Monsieur Héger's Pensionnat in Brussels, it cannot be said that she was a social success. The girls giggled at her queer clothes. Mrs. Jenkins, the chaplain's wife, stopped asking her to the house on Sundays, the girl was so odd, so silent. The daughters of a Dr. Wheelwright would have liked to go about with Charlotte, if only dull Emily could have been left behind.

She returned home, baked the bread, walked on the moors with her dog, and in the evenings was enveloped in the dusty, voluminous conversation of good old Mr. Brontë.

Then, soon after Branwell's death, the family knew that she, too, was dying. They would have liked to come a little nearer at that hour, but did not know how. They loved her, but nobody had ever understood her. How should they? She was not a creature of this warm human life, her home was not built with hands.

EMILY BRONTË 1818-1848

GEORGE ELIOT
MARY ANN EVANS 1819–1880

'A QUEER THREE-CORNERED GIRL, SALLOW AND dark' (to quote the mother's description of this disconcerting offspring), Mary Ann Evans, when aged thirteen, appeared so mature that she was mistaken for a twenty-five-year-old acquaintance, and a fellow school girl said that it was impossible to imagine she could ever have been a baby.

A homeless creature, longing for spiritual contacts, her life and work were woven on the same pattern: a certain heaviness and inelasticity together with a true nobility of outlook. These were her main characteristics, with that life-long search for 'something that would link together the wonderful impressions of this mysterious life, and give her soul a sense of home in it.'

She had moments of inconsistency. In youth she renounced the intention of attending an Oratorio because she could not decide on 'the propriety or lawfulness of such exhibitions of talent'; she could not believe that 'a pleasure that involves the devotion of all the time and powers of an immortal being to the acquirement of an expertness in so useless (at least in ninety-nine cases out of a hundred) an accomplishment, can be quite fine or elevating in its tendency.' Yet, two years after this pronouncement, she visited the Birmingham Festival, where the audience was considerably disturbed by her loud sobbing. The amusements and interests of her early years could not be described as light, or wanting in seriousness. Her first friends were a Mr. Bray, a wealthy manufacturer of ribbon, interested in phrenology, and the author of *The Education of the Feelings* and *The Philosophy of Necessity*, and Mrs. Bray, the author of a work on Kindness to Animals. This friendship resulted in Miss Evans becoming 'highly-strung,' and in her being beset by religious doubts. In 1843, however, she attended a public ball 'for the first and last time,' according to her biographer, Miss Haldane; who added: 'Perhaps because partners were scarce and the results disappointing.'

In 1851, after her father's death, her rather restricted social life broadened with her departure from Coventry to London, where for some time she lived in the boarding-house kept in the Strand by Chapman, the Editor of the *Westminster Review*, and his wife. Mary Ann Evans helped Chapman in certain literary matters and their friendship led to trouble with

Mrs. Chapman, but after a time this seems to have been smoothed over. It was at the Chapman's house that she met Herbert Spencer, who was then thirty-one, a year younger than Miss Evans.

It seems certain that at one time she fixed her affections upon Mr. Spencer, but he, though he remained her devoted friend, was unable to summon up any amorous feeling for her because (as he was careful to explain in later life) she was 'morbidly intellectual, a small brain in a state of intense activity. And besides, her nose was too long.' However, he confessed that he invariably found himself by her side at parties, and he undoubtedly conducted her to oratorios, conversaziones and other gaieties. Eventually this friendship led to Miss Evans making the acquaintance of George Henry Lewes, the literary editor of *The Leader* and the author of a *Biographical History of Philosophy*. Lewes had been deserted, years before, by a faithless wife who had left him with three children to look after, but divorce was, for some reason, impossible. This plain little man, deeply pitted with smallpox, was to Mary Ann Evans the dearest of all beings, and in 1854 she left England for Weimar with the man whom she regarded as her husband to the day when death took him from her. 'If there is one relation of my life,' she wrote later in a letter to a friend, 'which has been properly serious it is my relation to Mr. Lewes.' His sons (the eldest was nearly eighteen), called her 'Mother.' 'Let us all,' she wrote to him, 'father and mother and sons, help one another with love.'

And, indeed, their family life was one of constant devotion and a calm and certain happiness. In the midst of this happiness Mary Ann Evans found fame: she, whose first novel, published when she was nearly forty, was praised by Dickens and Thackeray, could not believe in the splendour of the new world opening before her. And how apt were, in most cases, the criticisms aroused by her works! It is true that *Adam Bede* was forbidden reading for young girls, but *Scenes from Clerical Life* called forth from Mrs. Carlyle the remark that Mr. Eliot (whose identity was then unknown) must be 'a man of middle age, with a wife from whom he has got these beautiful *feminine* touches in the book —a good many children and a dog! Not a clergyman, but brother or first cousin to a clergyman.

In later years the woman who, because of her irregular union, would never invite another woman to her house unless that invitation were sought: she who, when Lewes was commanded to the Court of Weimar, must be left behind, was so regarded that she 'dined at Mr. (Lord) Goschens, with a picked party, to meet the Crown Prince and Princess of Germany, Dean Stanley, etc.' Queen Victoria sent to make enquiries when she was ill. There were parties in the large house near

Godalming where the couple spent their declining years, and although, as an eyewitness wrote, 'it was rather an ordeal for most women to be called on to speak in a company so critical in nature, the hostess saw them through with the kindest expression on her face.'

In 1878, to her unspeakable grief, Lewes died. Eighteen months afterwards the lonely woman married J. W. Cross, the devoted friend of herself and of Lewes. She had at least this affection to lean upon; but not for very long, for on December the 22nd, 1880 she, too, died, and her loneliness without the long and faithful love of her life was at an end.

I find it difficult to read her works at this time. But it must be said that she covered homeliness, the common road, the working day, with a dusty gold. And it is possible to love a woman who could write, after the French Revolution of 1848: 'I would consent to have a year clipt off my life for the sake of witnessing such a scene as that of the men of the barricades bowing to the image of Christ who first taught fraternity to men.'

FLORENCE NIGHTINGALE
1820–1910

FLORENCE NIGHTINGALE, DAUGHTER OF A RICH father, was born to a life of unbraced comfort and uselessness. But she had the temper of fine steel and a noble contempt for 'angels without hands.' Throughout her life she fought relentlessly against stupidity, smugness and self-righteousness on behalf of the unfortunate, the poor, the forsaken.

'Hers,' wrote Sydney Godolphin Osborne, who visited her in the Crimea, 'was a post requiring the courage of a Cardigan, the tact and diplomacy of a Palmerston, the endurance of a Howard, the cheerful philanthropy of a Mrs. Fry. Miss Nightingale fills that post.'

'She had,' he said, 'an utter disregard of contagion. I have known her spend hours over men dying of cholera or fever.'

This was the woman who, having trained as a nurse, three years previously, against her family's wishes, set out for the Crimea in October, 1854, at the head of thirty-eight members of her profession.

At Scutari she found a hospital whose conditions were more appalling than those of the worst slums in Europe; built above open sewers, whence the foul air drifted into the wards, and with little or no bedding, surgical appliances, medical necessities, or possibility for invalid cookery. 'The vermin,' wrote Miss Nightingale to Sydney Herbert (January 4, 1855), 'might, if they had but unity of purpose, carry off the four miles of beds on their backs, and march with them into the War Office, Horse Guards, S.W.' Cholera and other fevers raged.

Florence Nightingale, on her feet for twenty hours out of the twenty-four, left, as she and her nurses were left, without rations for ten days, and for the rest of the time 'without food, necessarily,' could yet say, 'In the midst of this appalling Horror (we are steeped up to our necks in blood) there is good, and I can only say, like St. Peter, "It is good for us to be here," though I doubt if St. Peter had been here he would have said so.'

Hundreds of letters reached her from the mothers of the dying men she succoured. 'In order that you may know him,' wrote one mother, 'he is a straight, nice, clean-looking, light-complexioned youth.' 'Died in hospital, in good frame of mind,' was Florence Nightingale's docket for her reply.

Her task in the Crimea done, she returned quietly

FLORENCE NIGHTINGALE
Detail from the pencil drawing by Sir George Scharf, 1857

to England, avoiding the crowds that would have welcomed her. In England other tasks awaited her. She was instrumental in bringing about the reform of nursing in Workhouses; this, with the East London Society for Providing Sick Nurses for the Poor, the Government Department for Public Health, Civil and Military Hospitals for India, are only a few of the reforms and institutions we owe to her. Indeed, what does not the modern state of nursing owe to that fiery and great soul, so controlled and heroic, to that cold and lucid, constructive will?

Her life was saddened by the death, in 1861, of her friend and co-worker, Sydney Herbert. The work which was her glory and his pride continued. Honoured and beloved, when she was a very old woman, losing her sight and memory, the Order of Merit and the Freedom of the City of London were bestowed upon her. 'Too kind,' she murmured. Her 80th birthday was celebrated throughout the world by kings and nurses and those whom she had benefited. When she died, at the age of ninety, the offer made of a burial in the Abbey was refused. The heroine of the Scutari Hospital was buried simply, as she had lived, borne to her grave by six soldiers of the Army she had served so faithfully.

CHRISTINA ROSSETTI 1830–1894

WHEN CHRISTINA ROSSETTI WAS THREE YEARS old her father described her in a letter as 'walking all alone in the garden, like a little butterfly among the flowers.'

This should have been the life of this exquisite poet, who was not born to walk in the colder shade: the lovely dust on the wings of the butterfly was the only dust she should have known.

Christina Rossetti's interest in the life of the church weighed too heavily upon her poetry, which should have moved lightly and quickly always, a creature of nature, not red in tooth and claw, but running sweetly across the sunlight and summer shade like a bird. Poverty was too dull and dark a weight, ill-health cast a winter shadow. Above ball, the church numbed her spirit, for she had saintly habits and a saintly outlook, but she had not the irradiation and fire of the saints: her religion cast a cold clay upon her. *Goblin Market*, perhaps the most perfect poem written by a woman in the English language, this is the work of her nature—not the slow, dim, clay-cold verses of her religious life. *At the Convent Threshold* has passion of a sort, but it is a wry passion and discoloured.

The sweetness and charm which are the blood and sap of her poetry flowed long before she had come to ripeness. In the verses written when she was between fifteen and sixteen and printed by her grandfather, Polidari, at his private press, there is the sweetness of

> 'Roses, lilies, jessamine
> And the ivy ran between
> Like a thought in happy hours.'

And those hours were many, though poverty was always present. When her father, a refugee from his native Italy, began to lose his eyesight and could no longer continue his work at King's College, her mother went out to work. Her elder sister Maria, aged seventeen, became a resident governess, but was so unhappy separated from her family that she soon returned to them, and gave daily lessons instead. Gabriel, studying painting, could earn no money. But William, that saintly and sweet character whose whole life was given to his family, to providing for their needs and bearing their worries—William, who scarcely allowed himself the right to individual happiness—began, at the age of fifteen, to shoulder his life's burden and entered the Inland Revenue office as a clerk.

In.youth, Christina had the calm and thoughtful beauty of a Lippo Lippi Madonna. She often sat as model for her brother Gabriel, and she was also the model for the figure of Christ in Holman Hunt's *Behold, I stand at the door and knock*. But she was shy and diffident, and her silences seem to have been disconcerting.

When she was sixteen Christina fell in love with a friend of her brother, a young painter of inferior talent, James Collinson, the son of a bookseller at Mansfield. But this rather unattractive young man soon became a Roman Catholic, and Christina, to her grief, felt herself obliged to break off her engagement.

The peaceful family life must have been disturbed when, in 1849, Gabriel fell violently in love with Elizabeth Siddal. This radiant but unhappy creature, of an unearthly beauty, made no attempt to be on terms of friendship with Gabriel's family. Christina was accused by Gabriel of not appreciating Elizabeth, whose superior smile and pretentions as both poet and painter, coupled by the fact that the pretentions were upheld by Gabriel's friends, must have been trying to Christina. In addition, Elizabeth was now Gabriel's model and he no longer needed Christina. The moment came when Gabriel asked his friends not to invite Christina when he and Elizabeth were to be of the party.

Yet when Elizabeth took her tragic way out of life, and Gabriel's long descent to the depths began, it was to Christina, as well as to his mother, that Gabriel turned for comfort.

In 1860 Christina met, for the first time, Charles Cayley whom she loved to the end of her life, but whom she would not marry because Cayley's poverty would have been an additional burden upon the already overladen William (although that unselfish being was eager to shoulder it). There were, in addition, religious reasons which made the marriage impossible. But this gentle, sweet-natured, unsuccessful, shabby, vague creature lived in the heart of Christina Rossetti long after that dreadful day in December, 1883, when he was found dead from heart disease, in his rooms.

1860 and 1862—these were, perhaps, the happiest years of Christina's life, for in 1862 *Goblin Market* was published and, in spite of Ruskin's gloomy prognostications, had a certain amount of success.

But her life was soon to be overcast. When she was about forty she was attacked by Bright's Disease, which ruined her beauty as well as her health. In 1874 William married Lucy, the daughter of Madox Brown, and although Christina and her mother remained for a while in the family home, that arrangement soon came to an end. Mrs. William Rossetti, who was an agnostic, was irritated by Christina's church-going and religious conversations, she had no patience with that great artist's nervousness—for was she not, too, an artist? Had she not studied painting, and written a Life of Mary Wollstonecraft? Why must more allowances be made for Christina and her crotchets than for her own?

Old Mrs. Rossetti and Christina, to William's grief, removed to Torrington Square, where they were joined by Mrs. Rossetti's sisters. Here they remained until one by one the old ladies faded away. Maria had died long since, and Gabriel. Only William and Christina were left – the great poet and the beloved and faithful brother who had been the life-long staff on which she leant, and who was to survive her.

CHRISTINA ROSSETTI WITH HER MOTHER
Chalk drawing by Dante Gabriel Rossetti, 1877

ELLEN TERRY
Oil painting by G. F. Watts, 1864

ELLEN TERRY 1848–1928

THIS EXQUISITE BEING, GOLDEN AND WARM, ABOUT whose art there was nothing supernatural, declared: 'If it is the mark of the artist to love art before everything, to renounce everything for its sake, to think all the sweet human things well lost if only he may attain something, do some good, great art, then I was never an artist. I have been happiest in my work when I was working for someone else.'

What were the highlights of that life which was so radiant for all its sorrows, its cares? What were the secrets of that art which was a quintessence of her powers of living? It was as natural to her as the perfume is to a flower, and yet was the result of thought as well as of instinct. For behind that beautiful, slightly irregular face was an acute brain. She was a shrewd judge of acting and of people.

What, then, were those highlights? That evening when an eight-year-old child, the daughter of parents who were both actors, played Mamillius in Charles

Kean's production of *A Winter's Tale* and was applauded by Queen Victoria and Prince Albert: the day of her marriage to Mr. Watts, the great painter, who told his sixteen-year-old bride not to cry because it would make her nose red: the days that followed in Mr. Watts's beautiful house, where he was visited by Swinburne, and by Tennyson (who was always kind to her), by Gladstone and Disraeli—and the beautiful ladies who ruled the household and Mr. Watts told the child-wife she was not to talk: the day of sadness and humiliation when she knew that, through no fault of hers, the marriage was ended.

These were her memories, with the sadness and joy of her life with Edward William Godwin (the architect and initiator of an aesthetic movement in theatrical designs), the life of cooking, washing the two children born to them, to which she devoted herself and for which she cut herself off from her family and the stage. Then came her return to the stage, driven by poverty, then the bitter grief of her parting from Godwin. She married twice in after years, but those marriages could not mean the same to her as the dear companionship for which she had renounced so much. They meant to her safety, a reconciliation with her family, a home for her children.

When she was very old, and lived in her memories, was it of these years and moments of the past that she thought, or of the time when, as Portia, she swept London like a fire, and everybody, as she said, was in love with her?

Did she think of her triumphs as leading lady to Irving, of her affection for him (and her occasional irritation), of her friendship with Mr. Bernard Shaw, the friendship of two people talking across a distance? Or was it of the hard work that she thought, of the infinite study, with nothing left to chance? For it was not only chance that gave her that flavour, that radiance, that perfume—though she owed to her own nature her secret of swift and animal-like movement, her stillness that was like that of a flowering bough, and her honey-eyed sweetness. She was the child of instinct and of intellect.

GERTRUDE BELL 1868–1926

'IT WAS RATHER INTERESTING,' MISS BELL TOLD HER father, Sir Hugh Bell, after her attempt to climb the Finsteraarhorn in 1902, 'to see the way a mountain behaves in a snowstorm, and how avalanches are born, and all the wonderful and terrible things that happen in high places.'

That passage is the keynote of this extraordinary life of magnificent adventure and achievement. She did indeed see the wonderful and terrible things that happen in high places.

The granddaughter of Sir Isaac Lothian Bell, Bart., F.R.S., scientist, colliery owner and ironmaster, she had the scientist's curiosity and the business man's practicality. Scholar, historian, archæologist writer on art, mountaineer, explorer, gardener, naturalist, and distinguished servant of state, that boundless curiosity and strong commonsense were exerted in all these walks and flights of life. She was, by reason of her faith, courage and integrity, the spiritual sister of such

GERTRUDE BELL 1868-1926

men as Captain Oates and Colonel Lawrence.

The information amassed during her expedition to Hayil early in 1914 (this was but one of her numerous explorations) was of inestimable value to Britain during the last war, when Hayil was on the enemy side. In November, 1915, she was called to Cairo at the urgent request of Dr. Hogarth, who was in collaboration with Lawrence, because of her vast knowledge of the Northern Arabian Tribes.

'When,' wrote Lady Bell in the epilogue to her edition of her step-daughter's Letters, 'the crowning sequel came to those days of desert adventure, when she saw her dream of the Arab resurgence turn to reality, she was at the throbbing centre of the events which led to the chaotic leap into history of the Kingdom of Iraq, with an Arab prince on the throne.'

From Baghdad, in 1918, she had written to her father, 'I had a warm feeling of being part of it all, and so I am, you know, just as much as I am part of English surroundings. It is a curious sense to have two native lands, and to be wound into this one as that by long links of association.'

VIRGINIA WOOLF
1882-1941

A SHORT WHILE AGO THIS EXQUISITE BEING, WITH the sensibility of Dorothy Wordsworth and the talent of Jane Austen, was still with us. She was allied to many things in nature; she had the profundity of a deep well of water. But when she was talking, and listening to the talk of others, you felt she was like a happy child chasing butterflies over the fields of an undying summer. Only there was no cruelty; she would catch the lovely creatures for a moment, see the colours on their wings, and then set them free again, their beauty undimmed.

There was no happiness that you could not imagine her sharing, nor could you ever guess that there was a shadow in the world. Brave and shining, darkness could have no part in her.

After her tragic death a friend wrote of her that she had 'an unearthly beauty.' I would have said 'an unworldly beauty,' for part of her delightfulness lay in the fact that she enjoyed earthly things. Her beauty was great and she had the kind of unconscious elegance of some tall thin bird, with its long legs and delicate feet, and wondering turn of the head. With this she had a charm which had occasionally an innocently mischievous character, like that of a child.

In conversation with her, everything became exciting. She made thoughts fly to and fro more quickly. She had a swift and flashing sympathy like that which Dorothy Wordsworth must have possessed, her luminous mind lightened and heightened all subjects. Equally enchanting as talker and listener, she encouraged the conversation of her friends, she teased them gently, clapping her hands with pleasure and excitement when they scored some point. She was never tired of questioning; but questions were never wearisome when she asked them, for they led somewhere and often made the answerer see a new truth.

Such was her personality: and her work and her character were indivisible. Hers was a work more of radiance than of fire. It had no quality of danger in it. The beings in her novels and in that enchanting work, *The Common Reader*, are living creatures: we meet them as we meet our acquaintaßnces, they talk with us, laugh with us. I do not think that they tell us the secrets of their hearts. But then, many charming beings are unravaged by passions, undevastated by fires in the heart. They do not live dangerously, the great

VIRGINIA WOOLF
Chalk drawing by Francis Dodd

adventures are not theirs. But the flying happiness of the hour, the light on the wings of the bird, the dew on the morning world: these she seemed to hold in her long and beautiful hands, and as she touched them for a moment they became more real to us and it seemed that they must be unfading.

colour plates

Mary Sidney, (1561–1621)

Sarah Jennings, (1660–1744)

Lady Hester Stanhope (1776–1839)

Elizabeth Fry (1780–1845)

Grace Darling and her father saving the
shipwrecked crew

George Eliot (1819–1928)

Christina Rossetti (1830–94) with her mother

Ellen Terry (1848–1928)

black & white illustrations

Catherine Blake
Elizabeth 1 (1533–1603)
Queen Anne (1665–1714)
Esther Johnson (1681–1728)
Elizabeth Linley (1754–1792)
Sarah Siddons (1755–1831)
Mary Wollstonecraft (1759–1797)
Dorothy Wordsworth (1771–1855)
Lady Hester Stanhope's Residence at Djoun
A Quaker woman *c.* 1815
Jane Welsh Carlyle (1801–1866)
Thomas Carlyle (1795–1881)
Grace Darling (1815–1842)
Emily Brontë (1818–1848)
Florence Nightingale (1820–1910)
Gertrude Bell (1868–1926)
Virginia Woolf (1882–1941)

Index

Acknowledgments

PRION HAVE ENDEAVOURED TO OBSERVE THE LEGAL
requirements with regard to the rights of suppliers of
illustrative material and would like to thank Hulton
Getty Picture Library for its generous assistance.